T0158638

smoothie

CLAUDINE
TOUTOUNGI

CARCANET

First published in Great Britain in 2017 by
CARCANET PRESS Ltd
Alliance House, 30 Cross Street
Manchester M2 7AQ
www.carcanet.co.uk

A CIP catalogue record for this book is available
from the British Library: ISBN 9781784104122.

Printed and bound in England by SRP Ltd.

The publisher acknowledges financial assistance
from Arts Council England.

CONTENTS

SMOOTHIE

Because I think you'd like me better as an artefact
I sit for ages in the sculpture park.
Flies settle on my arms.

Because I think you'd keep me close if I'd been customised
in a foundry, I will myself to turn to bronze.
Rain falls.

J'ai la verticale
dans mon esprit I tell my spine,
channelling Matisse.

This is *not* a fad, like the long weekend I spent
being Danish in monochrome knitwear,
saying *tak* in exchange for tea,

this is for real. I shall remain here,
unmoved by sheep and hedge trimmers,
until you notice me.

HIJACK

Jump-cut to Rome and it's fast:
a hand on the throat, a *commedia dell'arte* gasp.
She is being spoken by the language Italian.

He stalks her in sunglasses.
For the length of an aqueduct, from the cool of a bar,
he flutters her hands, arches her brow, rolls her *r.*

On the Spanish Steps, the ghost of a touch,
a fleeting laugh. She spins round but
her English full stops are gone

and the way we say *dog eat dog* won't come
and back at the flat familiar phrases and tenses are packing for home.
The language Italian pours forth her sorrow

then stills her in close-up. She's stricken but only as Loren or
Lollobrigida do stricken: wildly, accusing the world
with dolorous shoulders and eyes.

Later, a candle between them cuts through the dark.
He calls her *Carina.* She only smiles.
Lupo mangia lupo; his voice is a ruin.
As he traces her cheekbone, she sighs.

MIDTOWN ANALYSIS

after Lorca's A POET IN NEW YORK

Some of those edge-of-the-precipice
people are circling,

smiling at breasts,
asking directions to places of worship.

Sunlight glares through gaps in metal towers.
You are always walking

towards the Norman Foster building.
Men rise again

from a hole in the street.
A red hand flashes.

You reach for a cocktail,
swallow a cab.

The Stock Exchange is not yet
covered in moss,

but everyone's timing is off.
The sense of scale is mortifying.

A man wants to explore your bag /
your heart / your mind.

You lie upside down on his couch.
Vermont Clothbound Cheddar fills your throat.

He blames the axial
pull of the vertical.

You choke. He suggests
you try to be less literal.

KHAMSIN ON BAYSWATER

The sand that's in my eye blew in from Africa.
And sand's a form of grit – that much I know.
And grit makes pearls that lovely fashionistas
take out for strolls along Bayswater Road.

I've no such milky jewel of clarity
to pierce the darkness, translate this din.
I test an Arab curse learned from my father:
May all of Egypt piss on this khamsin –

may all the sand contained in the Sahara
rinse itself down some infernal sink –
for coming right when nobody required her,
when every path's distinctly indistinct

except one path – the road to anarchy.
Remember Günter (was it Eich or Grass)?
Be sand not oil in the world's machinery.
Your words now. Say that, should someone ask.

NIALL

i.m. Niall McCabe

In the space between two worlds
I poach an egg. It's early.
I have fasted all night, a long night,
spent mainly talking with my spirit guide,
or rather, listening.
And when I say spirit guide, I mean
Niall, the Omagh boy from drama school,
who used to be all thunder in the pub.

He wore his cloud mass like a crown,
daring you to come and try and break it,
but in the dream, if he was weather,
he was a gulf stream,
he was a golden O reciting Shakespeare
in a parlour room with chintzy decor.

Once I was afraid to catch his eye during a love scene,
but in the parlour room we gazed and gazed.
No one could look away.
Of course, I begged him, 'How do you do it, Niall?'
because, in truth, I was desperate for his secret,
I was parched for his charisma,
but I couldn't hear his answer.

Still it was enough to see him back again and shining
resplendent in that parlour room,
after his miserable December passing.

You read too much   watch non-stop movies   after a time Jack Nicholson's fore-
head   wrinkles into Jean-Pierre Bacri's eyes and then you're quoting Carver in the ad
breaks   *He said it doesn't look good*   All this to stave off fugue states and
a sense of multi-platform loneliness   If only experts in the field of neuroscience
could formulate a mode of languishing in   dark rooms   trembling   a taste for noirish
verses candles absinthe   while   all the time ensuring   via tablets or a serum
behind the eyes   a breakthrough sensation   the purest pain-free pain

BOLTER

I can see why you would.
You're equine enough for starters. Shall we say jerky?
A fine, thoroughbred sort of jerk, twitchy as hell, with a long trail of
                                                    turf in your wake.

You look down on me from your high place, Emperor of Horses,
ears cocked for thunder and your eyes,
your eyes are two-thirds lid.

They do and do not shut me out.
Their single line of light
my stern reminder –

Don't pat this one. Don't feed him sugar.

SKIRTING

Somewhere,
potentially a roof terrace or gazebo,
preferably a contained space with a certain quantity of sunlight
bleaching the architecture,
two people are skirting the issue.

They skirt well,
not like an eagle skirting
thermals, but with old-fashioned grace
and an out-and-out commitment to enjoying the skirting

as long as the light trickles through the gothic
lattice and strokes the petals of the clinging
roses (old Europeans or hybrid perennials).

Elbows are involved.
Eyelashes are central.
A shoulder will slip
free of material at some key point.

Ideally, a butterfly grazing an ear
permits an intake of breath
or tense hiatus,

but if climate change or an increase in
urbanisation has put an end to fluttering,
if nothing is left in the air, save a trace of jasmine,

the skirting will still grow more urgent,
dextrous. It will ricochet.
It will become the butterfly.

DEAR MRS WILMOT

It was nice last year but do not come back here.
They found your cousin's slipper floating on the stairs and some untouched
rollers in a bag.
Something has caught us up.

I cast aspersions on the season's mental health. July took its revenge.
There used to be rain and some sun. Now there is just rain.
Now I am up to my neck.

The next flotilla won't be of boats. They're sending traffic cones.
Less fuss. My only hope's a flexible approach.
I'll pour myself inside.

Planted on high ground, you'll see me
eyeing the stars from my pod, an unripe alien.
Pray that the mother ship finds us.

The Linguisticator meets you at Carrefour.
Un vrai galant, he buys you *rouge à lèvres*.
Teaches socially accepted forms of extrication.

If someone gropes you, say *Arrête tes bêtises.*
If someone wonders why your hair is mussed, say *C'est le mistral.*
If someone asks you to admire their ugly baby, say *Je me sauve* and leave.

The Linguisticator is a veritable language experience.
You programmed him in Oregon but he caught a virus.
Now his Frenchness is *cent fois* off the spectrum.

Sings Aznavour as you tour the *centre historique* and Piaf on the tram;
Padam, Padam, when it clangs.
The Linguisticator can stop a tram with one raised eyebrow,

one *soi-disant* eyebrow. A fatalist, he has abandoned caution
with certain potent liquors of the region. Ask him if he's OK, he'll say
Le silence éternel de ces vastes espaces m'effraie.

Ask him what irony means, he says
Tout pour le mieux dans ce meilleur des mondes possibles.
But if his ennui peaks, he suspends all conversation.

Broods for hours muttering *Putain,*
je suis rien qu'un two-bit trompe l'oeil.
Malaise on a loop. It never fades.

say in a penthouse   say with glass walls   around 3 AM   the city
a drinks tray laced with shots   begins its revolutions   ice wine kahlua
schnapps   another gulp   another flash   ungrasped   golden ruby
amber   each stain as if it's medical   something you never
knew was there has been removed   and it winds you
holds you fast against the pane   your mouth a dumb show shaping
an address   to that siren shrieking voodoo
in the air

after resigning sat around
drinking Oolong tea
on their sunloungers.

How they'd laughed
trussing up
the inspector

for bouts
of white noise
over seventeen hours

(Lyons was clicking
the mouse. He never could
stick to a schedule),

but in truth, the whole
orchestration
had been full of holes –

administering shocks
to guards who had helped them,
slathering muck over all the wrong cars.

Oh nightmare logistics!
And nobody thanks you
for taking the pains.

They freshened the pot
with meds of their choice,
until somebody said

Enough. We did
what we could. Time
for some golf.

It seizes me
like the way, as a kid, I would fling open the door to the
downstairs cupboard
where we stored loo rolls
to give my best rendition of
The sun'll come out tomorrow.
I believed *This Is Your Life* filmed everyone
upwards of six, for future posterity.
I planned on lots of future posterity so
did my best Fat Sam into a cereal bowl,
saving my particularly heart-wrenching
Fantine for waits in car parks and
a shower cubicle in Wales.

Now I want each word to you
to be as much a knockout;
tender, but funny,
poignant, but droll,
in case it's all there is.
Terrible to end on
The flush has gone or
The damp's back or
something about the wrong tax code.
Terrible enough to put off
Actual Conversation.
Instead I leave you

gnomic, pre-planned voicemails
intended to uplift and edify.
*You must be able to extract
nutrient from a sandpit*, I try,
murdering Thoreau, and
Where there is nothing, there is peace.
You call and ask me to stop.
It's taken years for me to work it out.
There are no cameras.

PISS-POT

after Muldoon after Coleridge

What a beautiful thing it is, in a pot, urine.
If I was out of here, I'd bottle it.
Why not? It's organic. Honest.
The smell of all of us.

Nobody calls a spade
a spade these days. I would.
I'd stick it in a fancy jar. Give it a name like
Eau de Toilette. I'd rake it in.

Sometimes I have to look at it for hours.
Sometimes I think I'll drink it.

CATS BREAKFASTING

after John Craxton's painting CRETAN CATS

The meat of the fish is long gone.
Its smiling bones intersect with the back of a chair,
laid out pat, one more rung in a stack
and the velvety cats can't leave it alone.

There's no word for this in the language of cat,
this pawing furore, vertiginous spitting,
cats here then there, then not here and not there,
a hair's breadth between them and their skeleton love.

Tails, bones, chair, paw, they are spinning and the picture is
spinning, as they hiss in their fit, little beasts,
wild for the flesh of it, leaping in tempera strokes,
implacable button-blue eyes driven so strong
they could lick the egg yolk from the paint they're made from.

Instead of telling us how Manet
liked to hear his wife play
piano for their camarades

or riffing on the ways in which
syphilis imbued his work
with renewed vigour

or illustrating how Velázquez
is at the beating heart
of all his portraits –

the audio guide has begun to malfunction.

It flashes up a cartoon smiley
when it should be showing
Edouard's domicile

and when Julian Barnes starts to extemporise on how the world was
shocked by the
many gradations of black in his picture of Zola

a distinct series of raspberries can be heard,
blown softly in the background.

It culminates in a burst of Public Enemy's
'Fight the Power'

and the words *Do you like this nice life?*
floating gaily on the small handheld screen.

SLANT

Please place my sideways self in your arms
croons the tree to the beck

I've inclined your way for so long

your tendrils
astound me, your gusts, your lickety-spit

rages – all these years I've beheld them aloof
can't veer or flit from you

zounds you're a hoodlum

I would lay myself flat on your rocks, your slape rocks,
if you'd only leave off dashing past and away down Sour Milk Ghyll

I would bathe in you, I, your unswerving fanatic

I would do that for you –
swoon

A gull takes me to the edge of the town.
It is only grey here; great slates of it
and the roll and smash of sea into stone.

What must he have thought? No hint
of orange blossom, not a palm in sight
and all the light drained from the sky.

The northern tales as strange as tides,
like the Newtown Boggle disguised as a loaf
till a foolish lass took him home to toast.

And what of the olive trees, the spices
on the wind, the boulevard lovers?
No one can be a *flâneur* in the mist.

Against the railings, the ocean holds me.
Spray soaks my face. I breathe it in,
leaning towards my father's country.

REHABILITATING THE UNDERDOG

Do not discourage the underdog in his use of positive psychology.
He who looks in the mirror and habitually hears *mangy old mutt, no good
pound-hound, mud-loving, dirt-grubbing, dumb-ass beast* needs a
new mantra.

He who feels the ache of his choking dog-heart
or who looks down the barrel of his tail to see mile after
mile of bristling iron-filing fleas, must be taught to work
through his anger.

Let him howl at the moon for years,
feel the salt tears slide down his sad hanging face,
slobber and drool over wounds accrued through a life of
being trod on

and when all's said and done let him find a new
tongue in his skull and with it intone: *You ain't nothing but a
wise dog, wise dog, wise dog,*
until he believes it,

until he knows his bite is worse than his bark,
that he can learn new tricks,
that there's nothing to fear from the dark.

EXAMINER'S REMARKS

PART ONE

I am a precision marker. (It used to make Ruth smile that I would
cry out at the sight of a skilful clause.)
I will reward a range of complex sentences. Of course you may request
                                          a re-mark
(see footnote) but know that grades, like aspirations, can be lowered.
Obey the rubric. I cannot apply the mark scheme for descriptive writing
                                          to the story of a
drug dealer who sees the light and ends up selling fruit.
Allowance will be made for tone, large handwriting, English as a second
                                          language,
hayfever, the time zone, dyslexia and on and on it goes – it makes me
sick to see the list of variables and anyway
if I'm marking after dark and the dog won't shut up because it's not
                                          been fed because
Ruth used to buy its food and it's just me and the hound now
howling into the night, then
no benefit of the doubt will be given.

PART TWO

Tether all ideas to facts. I recommend the image of a donkey secured by
                                          rope
to a post. The donkey has a little room to move but it can never wander.
Why's harmony so hard in life and not in metaphors?
I tried to talk it through, but *God,* you said, before you left,
you're a criteria machine. Well let me tell you Ruth, however much you
squeeze them there's always some damn candidate twisting and
turning like a feral cat resisting capture when you try to
place them in the appropriate box and you away now living in La
Manga so what's the sodding point?
I used to like that donkey.
I'd think of him munching on his grass and fall asleep.
Now all I get's the smell of
compost and the sound of hooves.

WINTER WOLF

I was in a
   hypnagogic state
      when he arrived /

I couldn't move.

I registered sound hazily as
         Father Christmas moving round the
               furniture / televisual rumbles

from the next-door fan of Japanese
        cartoons / the scud of branches
           unhinged by the storm.

No pawing at the door
       could be for *us*,
         not *this* night.

I was lulled –

so when I found the tree up-
      turned and scalped of needles, angels
         dismembered, presents gone,
             the carpet

studded with glass,

      I felt almost serene to see what I
         had missed – the long un-
           wished-for caller

come at last.

Mrs Schwarzkopf cannot get her window open.
It's rain out there, set in, buffeting –
but she wants freshness.

Last night there were no crêpes as advertised.
Mrs Schwarzkopf had the cheese.
She can cope with cheese,

with buffeting, with the conservatory
roof leak, the towel being frayed, the waiter
crimsoning with shame over

coffee that could rival ditchwater,
crackers soggy on first bite.
Is it *walk the tightrope* or *gangplank* here they say

to mean the English can be nervy,
often unamenable to scenes of direct confrontation?
In their vicinity Mrs Schwarzkopf finds

her facial muscles form a rictus
grin. It will be more effective if she grins.
No she does not want a cup of tea,

or small talk about the local
pudding. She wants the window
to be open. She wants the window to be open.

CAMEL

Today I would like to be a camel
I want the pride of a camel
I want the hauteur of a camel
not just the height of a camel
(though that would be good too)
but the sneer of a camel
I want to do disdain as only camels can do
I want to look down my nose knowing
I am not a common dromedary
I do not have one hump I have two
which makes me better than you.

When I exhale it shall be
slowly, wearily, against
a backdrop of magnificent dunes.
My breath shall call to mind
the sound of bees fizzing as they collect
a nectar they know
unquestionably is theirs.

MY MONSTER

My monster lies down in green pastures,
scoffs caterpillars off nasturtiums,
likes me to tickle his underside.

My monster burps and farts and
blows his nose on oily rags. His
laugh is hooves on cobbles.

They tried to cauterise my monster's
nose but he crunched the cautery kit
in his jaws, curious of silver nitrate.

I fear you cannot reform my monster.
His habits will not be reeled in for queens'
birthdays or ambassadorial visits.

When others file behind the cordon
my monster will be out and roaming,
prone to sniff the flanks of cows,

pick snails off flaking sills,
weep for a duck stranded on tarmac,
weep and weep until the duck swims free.

COLUMBA PALUMBUS

for Danielle

Seeing as I have escaped the loudly angry woman
itemising each and every ailment of the nation –
the failures, rents, lack of safeguards in the mechanism –

and seeing as in my ears now I have the rush of water from the civic
fountain,
I can kneel, press the soil, weighted only
by the munificently cooing wood pigeon

who would have me know it's better to *Take
Twooo Cows, Taffy, Take Twooo Cows,*
which feels today like wisdom

inexplicable and soft – the sort
Master Dōgen might impart if he were Welsh or
riddling with his devoted listeners.

it struck me –
the inscrutability of washing-labels
is just like you.
Fluent in a secret code.
Hidden meanings.
Ellipses…where…
the thread unravels…
Still, what cool authority.
A fragment promising
ultimate enlightenment
if only it can be deciphered
before the dye runs
before the stick man
with his hands held up in horror
at his shrunken boxers
reveals he's not a man at all
but the sign for
Do not tumble dry
in most South Asian countries.
Also here.
Idiot.
Probably everywhere.
Probably even in the Arctic
though they might not use it much –
too cold to undress much in the Arctic.
Also here. Apparently.
This one – from a shawl
you bought way back –
The small defects
in this object are the guarantee
of its authentic nature
– this one I cut out.
Leave on your pillow.

HOLIDAY

To some extent I am standing
on one leg in an icy creek,
watching the acute-angled beak of a nearby heron dip
down into salt-clogged seaweed
beds, where fish peep about as the sun
grows fat in the sky.

Then again I am also flat on my
front, lodged amidst white hotel sheets,
still, though I've swallowed the
sea and cannot stop moving, drugged by the
drag of its tides, rocked this way and that
by the sway of its waves, while you stare

wide-eyed into nothing,
waiting, wondering why I
don't speak.

Salutations dear one
the comfort / dazzle / fuel of your friendship
warms my heart

I am in fetters / tears / hiding
but you dear one
dear comrade / flower / lodestone of my past

you can spare me this bleak hour / hole / catastrophe
by means of money / love / drugs
please send with urgency

black clouds / crows / drones
fly high above our heads
but you dear Aniko / Gerhardt / Les

you alone can set me free
you are the flicker / candle / incendiary device
to light my dark

thanks I cling to you
like a person clings to hope before it's broken
into remnants / tatters / parts

Before Ed died, his fridge got hot.
Shrugging off its former life as one long
chilly charade it set itself to
tropicalise inside. Milk became
sludge, bacon putrid, alien white
spores landed on a dish of cooked tomatoes.
He tried to reason with it
but the only sound it made was
fast and mean: *Ribbet. Ribbet.*
Like a frog on acid. Like it liked to leak
sedition to the yard outside,
where the birds no longer woke up singing,
only lay around on branches,
smoking joints, bitching about the cats.

He went in one last time to
liberate a sausage pie.
It was hell in there. Noxious
geysers steamed in salad trays.
Froth drooled from condiment jars.
The coolant in this item's veins was molten.
It ticked, he thought, for joy.
I made you a bomb.
It's in the fridge, joked Ed.
Nobody laughed.

It's late   you've done your covert Ministry of Silly Walks impression
                   fourteen times around the concourse
                   contemplated shoplifting a Capri-Sun
                   sent a text containing more than seven instances of
                   lovely to your friend who met up with you,
                   because she met up with you.

It's late   the Irish lads are wheeling out their cocksure
                   quips. You tried the c-word in an act of
                   badinage. It bombed. The toilet woman in the
                   hi-vis jacket's going
                   rogue. She sets the automatic flush off
                   willy-nilly. People squeal.

It's far too late to regret earlier opting for a stab at funny over a stab at
                   kind. Ultimately it came out as
                   just a stab.

Also too late   to feel an affinity with moles, bowl-fish, soldiers, leashed
                   dogs and the male monal you met that time
                   in captivity –
                   sad bird. You stared
                   eyeball to eyeball.
                   It stalked its perimeter.

It's late   the lights are on in M&S but no one's
                   taking stock. Everything is copious
                   and alarming. Men dread the cold
                   clutch of dawn.

It's late   be grateful.
                   There's no blood on your lips or steel
                   in your gut.
                   The last train is coming.
                   It is coming from Biggleswade.
                   It is coming from Welwyn.
                   It's coming. It's crawling. It's here.

After the lobster salad, we eat gender-neutral snails.
This was Lucian Freud's neighbourhood, you say.
Mealy white buttocks crenellate the leather seat.
They did a knock-through. Even the car park now is
avant-garde. They sprinkle my linguini with particles
of stuffed Pomeranian. It leaves a chemical aftertaste.
You say, those who have left are long gone, those who
want to leave will, those who can't, won't. There's something
mothy, something mothish, something moth-eaten about
your aura. You say the waiter has *un oeil qui dit zut
a l'autre*. We order burgers – bison that has lived
without duress. I ingest drugs under the table.
Both of us are hoping not to make a nasty end.

Sprang a leak out there in Eastbourne.
Brain got claggy. Too much sun.
Rage at trippers (mainly Italian).
Rage at Debussy (so overdone).

Take out the birds with their coloratura.
It wheedles and curdles. Take out the waves
– that non-stop shalt/shalt-not on shingle,
the *va' fa' un culo* dropkick spray.

Take out the pier with its blistering timbers.
The fit-bits. The head-butts. The roaring lads.
The woman with the seagull titter.
The drifters. The fish heads. The *haves* and the *hads*.

Give me a room with a darkening shadow.
Hand me a pillow. Hand me a drug.
Bring down the blinds on the splintering shoreline.
Drain it. Transpose it. The sea is a thug.

is the part where the poet is accused of sophistry.
Insulting terms like *gift of the gab* appear in reviews
wildly dismissive of any attempt at meaningful content.

The poet takes to drink and solitude.
This was part of his life before but now stretches beyond the central
territories

colonizing all outlying atolls and archipelagos.

In a dark time, the poet notes, *the eye begins to see.*
Yes! he thinks. That's terse and sinewy. Chew on that!
Later he deletes it. Junks the file. Eats jam.

At the zoo he started to hope;
perhaps this would end in a wedding?
Look at the kindly way she fed the giraffe.
Such compassion was infectious! Call it a germ
he wanted to catch. He bought her a plant.
Driving home they sang along to Elvis on the radio.

He wanted to broadcast his joy on the radio
but instead he told his sister Hope,
who, not liking his girl, felt she should plant
a seed of doubt about the wedding.
Just a hint. The merest germ
of mischief: Wasn't it dangerous to feed a giraffe?

There are plenty of things that can kill a giraffe.
Peanuts. Candy. It could have choked and no one there to radio
for help. Even now what she fed it could have passed on the germ
of something deadly. Face it, the giraffe had no hope;
it wouldn't make it to the wedding
and would soon be pushing up a plant.

He regretted buying the girl a plant.
She'd been foolish, practically killing a giraffe.
What if there were animals at the wedding?
Would they be safe? He'd have to call that radio
psychiatrist, the one who handed out hope
like it was free, like it was a germ.

But the shrink was off. Instead the phone-in was on germ
warfare. In the event of an attack, plant
a kiss on your lover's lips and hope
like hell the wind turns. The giraffe
was not easy to bring into the radio
debate, so he started by talking about the wedding.

It was out of the question to think of a wedding,
said the experts. And the specialist in germ
conflict wanted, given the facts, to radio
through for intelligence on this girl. Could she be a plant
– driven by her anarchist buddies to wipe the giraffe
off the face of the planet? A sick joke from those who spat on hope?

The girl, tuning in to the radio, smashed up the plant.
There was now no hope of a wedding,
though no germ had in fact touched the giraffe.

Leaving aside the mountain pass
in the French novel you read
in one sitting to avoid my relatives
– the one where the shepherdess
drinks hemlock fatally at dusk –
leaving aside Aunt Marjorie,
her naked denial of sex and
insistence at all times on close proximity
to teapots, leaving aside my Moldavian
cousin's persistent tin-whistle renditions
of the theme from M*A*S*H and your
bouquet of impatiens, which irked
my mother, leaving aside the lot of them and
their protracted acts of passive
aggression, may I simply say –
Come again. Come often.

IF THE GENERAL DEMEANOUR OF
CHEERFULNESS INTERCEPTS A BULLET

it will leave a scar
and though great strides have been taken in modern plastics
that scar may turn septic
creating disfigurement
not something poetic like a crescent moon or the mark of a scythe
but sores, burns, holes, ruptures
– something so bad it asks to be masked,
not with a pale, light, *commedia* mask like our friend's in the musical
but a full-frontal veil
– black, heavy, all-obscuring.
We should tear it off.
Detonate our smiles.

RESTORATION

There may be jealousies even within your own family.
Some would prefer you in pieces,
stoppered in jars or shrunk to the size of shabti –

reduced to a walk-on scrawl in your list of descendants,
your story rescinded, papyrus redacted and your big, fat
heart gobbled up by a ghoul with flat eyes.

Let them try. Let them cling to their version.
No flurry of wings to swoop in and save you,
no solar-charged chariot raising you up,

just dust and oblivion. Meanwhile in amulet fragments, orpiment, resin,
in Apis the bull on your footboard, faience and sycamore, ochre and
mud, there you are

cliffhanger –

you've lasted millennia
for those you know will make you whole again.

SOLO

– A jagged note,
torn, raw energy
not of eulogy
for the ball in the net,
more like a bricked-up,
screeching creature
skirling and freaking out
in a room where it's lost
its way.

She knows men
howl in this place.
Mousy, headscarved, unseen,
she sends forth
her gut-brewed roar
juddering wide,
the wildest sound
she ever made
for loss, for lack, for Chrissake,
for the ruckus of it.

All that's left's the sea,
but your mother told you
never stare at the sea; it steals minds.
This was in response to your concern that only insincere men could like
                                                                    you, so

as wisdom goes, it may have been unsound.
Still, you turn your back on the Atlantic,
and since the brown signs lead you nowhere
(the museum – rubble; the church – vanished)
lurk behind the lobby's potted palm,
eavesdropping on gabble:
Just the one wife here? could be *Is there Wi-Fi here?*
could be *Adjust your tie please, dear,*
if it were English,
which it isn't.
You let them seat you in the restaurant's
darkest corner – no serenader ventures near,
no gypsy selling roses.
You cultivate an air
of notoriety and when
the glances nearby harden,
retire behind your buttress
guidebook. Except, that candle can't afford you half the light
you need to read by.
Nothing for it but to turn him over
in your mind a few more times
like a holiday coin.
Look again. Look closely.
His jawline's far more plausible in copper.
And all around the edges
his message to you,
totally convincing
in the Latin.

APOSTROPHE

Tonight the white moon is as slim as a fingernail.
Slick as grammar, this slender curl,
the night sky's Apostrophe of Possession.

How easily it stakes its claim.
Cool ivory. Made by some celestial brushstroke,
one fell lick to say
There. That's mine.

How would it be if I could hook you with such certitude,
my arm curving around your shoulders?

Nobody questions the birds.
Their trills are never subject to inspection or
forced to satisfy requirements.

Light-boned libertarians
(the opposite of confidential),
they cannot keep it in.

You will not see them lining up in rows,
reeling off content-approved medleys
to a committee of creatures who know

nothing of song and who
certainly don't have wings.

GIANT RECUMBENT BRONZE

They call me Sunlight Totem.
Cool Flanks. Sheep-Gatherer.

They ask me was I always dappled,
my breasts so vast? How did I lose my arms?

They want to know about resilience,
if curves are arbitrary, they want to touch my three-dimensional knees.

They may not touch my three-dimensional knees.
They cannot comprehend my stillness.

Only the sheep,
huddled in the hollows where I sprawl

show prescience.
Lovely live-action monuments.

Conjugate the wisdom in their bleats:
shearing, sheared, shorn

THE WATCHER

after Mary Bonham-Christie of Brownsea Island

It was over scones the thought arrived: my creatures should roam free.
I rushed to undo bolts and tethers –
seeing finally a barnyard runt meant more to me than any human soul.

Now I let the scent of trees sustain me: mulberry, willow, cedar, yew.

After death some Buddhists give their bodies up for music –
thigh-bone trumpets, skulls as drums –
but I'm less use than air, snared within this wooden frame.

If this is penance for the crone I ditched on Poole Quay –
her and all the others booted off for butchery
and stealing eggs – I'll pay it.

I lived my days in lush misanthropy. I don't regret it.

At noon the heat grows heavy and the watchers droop.
On the lagoon, little egrets slush about the mud flats
and if I sigh you'll hear it when the hide slats creak.

Cooped up here, I pass the hours monitoring
the passage migrants: their to and fro,
the endless pulse of wings rising.

Sometimes I'd like a sentence.

I try for words.
Nothing comes,
only the sound of leaves, whispering.

THIS JUST IN

We strongly advise getting out of the house and talking to real people –
old people, young people, it doesn't matter which, so long as they are

people

not projections or aliases or dust.

There are many varied health benefits to talking to real people –
intestinal sugar content drops, purity of heart soars,
frequency of supra-ventricular ectopic beats declines.

When asked in a survey to equate talking to real people
with food consumption, 76% said it was like drinking a smoothie,
15% like discovering an old boiled sweet in your pocket, 9% mentioned

cramps.

There is currently a government study into talking to real people.
Knock-on effects will be plotted on graphs and peer assessed.
Some of the peers will be people, talking. Some of it will feel real.

I'm thinking of going to Honduras
riding the rail road there.
I was having a terrible time
before that thought. This girl
came up to me in the toilet
smiling – *I can't remember your name*
baring her teeth, telling me
an A-lister loved her
script, the way she pulled
off English gents (incisor
flash) but no, she couldn't
give me all the deets. *Mustn't*
jinx it (ferocious gleam). *And was I up to much?*
No? Well never mind. Close to a kind of mental
rape to pounce like that, barely
seconds after a discreet
pee and in the thick of flushes, taps and faulty soap
dispensers, exit barred by fit-
to-bursting women and her not stopping, even
at the hand dryers, even when the barrier
jams and the Do Not Slip sign
trips me – on and on, right up until the outer
limits of the concourse, which is why
I'm going to Honduras. Which is why
I should have gone.

WITHOUT MOORINGS

Yesterday when you were upset, I
wanted to tell you – things get
rubbed out all the time

faces, thoughts, lines of
communication. Take this empty space,
around which the artist has sketched

the beige sizzle of hot sand, the cry of an out-
of-sight gull, the breath of a sleeping child
sighing behind drawn-down blinds.

All the people in it have left, or died, or
are in hiding and even the unmanned boats go nowhere,
save for one without moorings

nosing towards freedom
on a fishless sea.

REINDEER

translated from the Evenki

the man who has spilled his urine under that tree
            has fulfilled my desire for salt   partially
(it cannot be fully)
           after salt there is only the prospect of more salt
to propel me   twenty miles
    upstream   more   at six miles an hour   to find salt
if I arrive and   – no salt   I will bash my head
    against bark   you say to dislodge bugs
       but really it's from lack of salt
remember the glory days with Master Shaman?
            our travels to the Upper Lands always involved salt
   (the Upper Lands have never-ending salt)
now it's usually a child who wants a ride   or stands beside me
                   without salt
I may get frazzled   I may stamp on its foot
       you think I'm ditzy but I'm not ditzy
I know the kick salt brings   the power   the loquacity

You're there in front of me
looking like the longest, tallest
coolest glass of water. You might as well have
Drink me written on your collar.
My heart swims in my chest like a fairground
goldfish trapped in plastic and
whether it's the fact we're gulping coffee
after coffee from the buffet, or that every time
you touch my elbow things feel worse, or the way
we don't make room for others in our conversation – I can't
tell, but it seems to me your tongue sticks to the roof of
my mouth, though it doesn't and I can't pronounce the
word I need to say and even when my friend, your wife,
arrives it doesn't come and so I say congrats. Not
even the whole word just its shrunken cousin –
and your expression hovers right before your face
but doesn't seem to want to land.

RETREAT

I have made my nest undercover
close to bark and bark's grasp and no other

treecreepers cannot reach me and the birds
far off are planetary

here I am
in the spyholes between leaves

touch and go if you'll see me emerge

THE CORRECTRESS

Did you ask for this, colossus of the classroom?
Statuesque in stacked mules and jewels at the ear,
such lambent pearls! Swaying a thousand
soaring states of consciousness.

Days spent laying down the fault-lines of fail and pass.
An edifice in lipstick. Rock-steady in the passing of decrees
and those hypnotic practised tones: *All the usual
rules apply, answer each question in every section, prioritise.*

Night-times you line up words the way you like them;
rhymes skittish (*laissez-faire, debonair*) and spiritual
(*assuage, sage*). You keep them locked in boxes,
precious moths whose wings will slowly dry.
Behind the eyes could something else be crumbling?
Don more mascara. Do not let them fly.

The eye stared up at you.
It was your eye,

naked, bargaining,
painted on the shell of something white and hard,

what dentists use for moulds, they said,
along with other words in cubicles

enucleate, sympathy reaction, orbital implant.
The eye stayed dumb but shone.

You felt it had some front,
the gleaming fake, with the upstart look.

Too late to back out now.
Too late to be let off the hook

by this newfangled
limpet, way too late to undo the loss

of your own strange planet,
milky white, protruding,

orbiting now only the afterlife,
a haze of blue ringing its rugby-ball shape.

In the absence of an eye there is only
a lack to be not looked into.

Think of it as a gum, they said but
honestly you'd rather not and instead

adopt celebrity tactics: headscarves, shades,
no mingling with the masses,

grateful beyond words for the eyelid's
smooth discretion.

When the day arrives
you confront the cool imposter,

suddenly soothed by his chutzpah. His sheer darn
polish makes you think it might work.

It feels like nothing, weighs nothing.
You hold your breath, holding the glass,

meet your face, as it once was
in a photo when you were small,

your smile, shy,
your ordinary symmetry.

COLD

After I brought it back from the ceilidh
where the lukewarm buffet did nothing
to dispel the arctic breeze coming up
the stairs of the Guildhall, a knifing breeze
straight into the heart of the dance,
I sat down in the kitchen and let it overpower me,
glorying in it, like a child waggling its tooth loose.
You were working and I, not wanting to disturb,
let its sea mist swamp me, whoosh, till I sneezed
with it, enjoying the tenor of my sneeze, its spit.
Where've you gone and got that from? you said,
like the culprit germ was rare, fished from some antique reef.
All is well, my dear. Look. I am curing it
with this morsel of chocolate reindeer.

MACHINE DREAMS

your fridge fancies a sauna

your iron longs to cross the Serengeti
smoothing desert wrinkles as it goes

your hoover wants to put its feet up on the sofa
eat snacks, make a few crumbs

your kettle hopes to sing live at the Met
The Queen of the Night, if possible

(your alarm clock yearns for a lie-in)

your hairdryer wants its neck to extend
to fly free as a swallow on a cool air current to a
hotter land where hair dries naturally

your smartphone, iPad and satnav discuss
Buddhist life in the foothills of Sri Lanka

how quiet the days must seem to those monks there

how soft the breath of those lush plants

When I first met you I was happy with your lies.
They were comforting and knowing they were
lies I enjoyed their artistry and narrative structure.

In the evening I would take a dental stick and pick
out bits of pear from in between my teeth. Every little
piece of pear flesh was usually another lie that made

me feel fizzy and slightly drunk. After our third encounter –
more nutritious lies – I went home and remembered
precisely what it was to be a child in bed doing fuzzy felt;

gorgeous and cocooned and Mistress of My Own Fate
Forever. Sometimes I take a Vitamin C late at night. A final,
virtuous act. I think about emailing you, saying – we're stuck,

but you're stuck the bad way. Me, I'm stuck
like the flamingos of the High Andes. The lake
they stand in may freeze overnight, but they know –

come morning – sun climbs, ice thaws, limbs don't snap.

The man I talked to said your
head came open like a soft-boiled egg,

the brains leaked out
in a herring-shaped stain,

but though I'd like to find your mark
upon the cliffside,

rocks, it seems,
are porous.

You've seeped away
to nothing,

to sea-spray, a bed-
and-breakfast rumour

retold at North Bay
where the sign advises:

Vacancy: Enquire Within.

Kitchen stank today. Bags overflowing with putrid rot. Recyclables in all the wrong bins. Grease. You had your *I can't clean, I'm a paraplegic* face on. You've been trying for hours to isolate the muscles in your little finger so it's the only thing that moves. You want to feel the pain? Feel this: your wife has dysentery, the cat starved, maggots roam our home.

CRAIG

The only one I speak to is Craig and
he's deaf and doesn't read lips.

People say the deaf make great listeners but Craig pulls
faces and makes obscene gestures.

I tell him all the ones I've slept with, their different lies,
who I'd like to send to their graves and how the others took and never gave.

I get to telling him how if I don't do something soon the
loneliness will kill me, which is when he gives the finger.

Give it a rest, he mouths.
Or I imagine he does.

THE LOCAL GODS

Hala is the god Horus come to earth as a tour guide.
She is birdlike, omniscient,
she knows the Aswan Dam's dimensions.

At Dendera a Japanese man throws up in the toilets and Hathor,
goddess of joy with the horns of a cow and his wife's face,
strokes his back.

Sky goddess Nut works the Abu Simbel flight these days.
She's coiled and formal as you board but sometimes, when alone,
her long, long limbs stretch out to tidy away peanut packets from the
                                                    back of the plane.

At the Papyrus Institute the usual girl is off so Maat, goddess of justice,
                                                    steps in.
Her feather of truth bobs when she bends to cut the plant.
Later she serves hot sweet tea and sees the pictures go for a fair price.

Sobek tears tickets at the Crocodile Mausoleum.
His jaws recede in gleaming points but he keeps his head robed
and no one sees.

Anubis has a job as an armed guard at the Esna Lock.
Rifle-clad, he lolls smilingly in the sun
but his silhouette does not smile.

LANDING

Before they emerged from their capsule
they never imagined birdsong or the sound
of the ocean crashing upon the shore.

The jerk of recognition it induced
in the pit of their spacesuits;
so many harmonies courting each other

across the coldest of stratospheres. And even if
it later proved a simulation, designed to reduce
cortisol in the bloodstream of long-haul voyagers,

no one could explain the salt on their lips,
the soft specks of sand on their lashes.

Now that I sleep well at night
and know I have
like Princess Alexandra of Bavaria before me
a piano lodged inside my gut
(though mine is not of glass),
swallowed whole
one late September evening, as a child,
I wear the baggy garb of the obese
without a qualm,
staggering sideways along streets,
on escalators pressed flat
against the wall
(no doubt a shambles, seemingly,
no doubt, crazed).

I was a pale and poxy girl.
A dog chased me in circles,
yapping at my skirt.
My brothers laughed. I cried.
The skirt ripped.
So the years passed.
Crunch. Yap. Rip.
Nothing sonorous.
Nothing spooling gorgeously
like Brahms
or Liszt
until I heard both for the first time in the civic hall,
played by a Soviet soloist so immense
I felt I'd died but been brought back.
I wanted to brush the ivories once for luck.
In the concert's after-hush
the auditorium gaped
at my insouciant approach.
I mounted the stairs,
close, so close,
but then I tripped

whilst falling *up*,
mouth open, like a goon,
downing the Steinway
circa 1892.

I felt better almost at once.
My skin improved. Dogs
stayed away, but the best came after years.
The booming hiss of the bee,
the stuck needle of the sparrow's
chirp, machinery, sirens, planes,
alarms, all the cackle this world hands
out for free, I absorb,
convert and am
transformed by.
Nothing inside
but resonance,
tremulous,
and not one
string is false.

Sunshine, you say, *is boring*, so you never see the light and all the bodies
falling; Celesti's muscular angel in the chapel, the French girl
doing underwater handstands, her legs endlessly
toppling back into the blue.

Who wants to walk through ruins in the heat at noon?
I do. Even if the light that hits the stones is biting.
Even if the stones reshape and shift
around me. A nose. A lion's paw.

Squares and slots of sunlight dance. I'm lost but can't
stop smiling at arteries of pillars, ledges, slabs that jut,
extend and almost touch, not in ending but
incipience.

This slate's alive and everything beside it's
paltry: You. Me. Hate. Love. My teeth. Our tiff.
The tiny sparrows. The spume of Garda spray
so far below.

The olive trees confirm it.
Branches gesticulate against the sky.
See this? Questa bellezza? they cry.
It stays. It dazzles. You die.

I would have forced you from the cliff if we had missed this
and walked in the olive grove afterwards. I could have written an ode.
On the way out I crush some rosemary in my fist.

SEPTEMBERISH

someone said   leave your rancour snagged on bracken
    inhale yellow woodsmoke
never mind   if the path to revelation's clogged with loosestrife, with
    Devil's-bit
    if the rock formation in your face begins to ache
this is nature   plain white-bread sky
    silver-washed fritillary uncalled to account
and you   your sporting rivalry with a down-at-heel sheep
    to see who'll climb the mountain slowest
oh ho   thinks sheep
    but you're as obdurate as that tractor in that ditch and
even if   you meet yourself halfway up already coming back
    (cagoule-less, Medusa-haired, stinking of weed)
keep on   in the rumination contest
    you can win

ACKNOWLEDGEMENTS

Grateful acknowledgements are due to the editors of the following publications, in which versions of some of these poems first appeared: *Poetry*, *PN Review*, *Magma*, *Poems in Which*, *The North*, *The Fenland Reed*, *The Literateur*, *New Poetries VI* (Carcanet, 2015), *Migration: The Compas Anthology* (COMPAS, 2014), *Alba*, *erbacce*, *The Delinquent*.

For their generosity, inspiration and unflagging spirits huge thanks to Rebecca Watts, Emma Harding and Adam Crothers. I'm indebted to the many whose willing ears have helped these poems arise. Warm thanks to David Fairweather, Ismahan Suleiman, Katherine Lucarotti, Laura Forster, Mark Waldron, Michael Schmidt, all at Carcanet and to my family for their love.